Joanne C. Wachter

Classroom Volunteers

Uh-Oh! or Right On!

Copyright © 1999 by Corwin Press, Inc.

All rights reserved. Use of the reproducible forms in this book is authorized for local schools and noncommercial entities only. Except for that usage, no other part of this book may be reproduced or utilized in any form or by any means, electronic or mechanical, including photocopying, recording, or by any information storage and retrieval system, without permission in writing from the publisher.

For information:

Corwin Press, Inc.
A Sage Publications Company
2455 Teller Road
Thousand Oaks, California 91320
E-mail: order@corwinpress.com

SAGE Publications Ltd.
6 Bonhill Street
London EC2A 4PU
United Kingdom

SAGE Publications India Pvt. Ltd.
M-32 Market
Greater Kailash I
New Delhi 110 048 India

Library of Congress Cataloging-in-Publication Data

Wachter, Joanne. C.
    Classroom volunteers: Uh-oh! or right on! / Joanne C. Wachter
  p.　cm.
  ISBN 0-8039-6880-9 (cloth: perm. paper)
  ISBN 0-8039-6881-7 (pbk.: perm. paper)
  1. Volunteer workers in education.　I. Title.
  LB2844.1.V6　W33　1999
  371.14′124—ddc21
                                                      99-6347

This book is printed on acid-free paper.

99　00　01　02　03　04　05　10　9　8　7　6　5　4　3　2　1

Production Editor: S. Marlene Head
Editorial Assistant: Julia Parnell
Typesetter: Rebecca Evans
Cover Designer: Wendy Hastings Coy

Contents

Preface	vi
About the Author	viii
1. Uh-Oh!	1
2. Thinking About Volunteers in a New Way	3
3. Setting Priorities	26
4. Recruiting Your Volunteer Staff	30
5. Training Volunteers	37
6. Maintaining a Smoothly Running Program	45
7. Showing Appreciation for Volunteers	56
8. Deciding Where to Go From Here	60
Reproducible Sheets	64

The Corwin Press logo—a raven striding across an open book—represents the happy union of courage and learning. We are a professional-level publisher of books and journals for K–12 educators, and we are committed to creating and providing resources that embody these qualities. Corwin's motto is "Success for All Learners."

Preface

Elementary schools are often blessed with eager parent and community volunteers. This situation is wonderful . . . if the volunteers are part of a well-thought-out program. Volunteers should make classroom programs easier, not harder, to run. But that is not always the case.

Why a Book on Volunteers?

Volunteer programs only run smoothly with careful forethought and maintenance. The challenge is that most teachers and administrators have never had any guidance or instruction in how to set up and run volunteer programs successfully. *Classroom Volunteers: Uh-Oh! or Right On!* is designed to provide the information that individuals, teams, and schools need in order to have outstanding volunteer programs. Not only does use of this book help fill in the missing gaps in information, but it also saves educators time by giving them ready-to-use plans and resources.

Who Will Enjoy the Book?

Classroom Volunteers was written with elementary educators in mind. It will be a valuable resource for individual teachers who use classroom volunteers. Its use may be even more exciting when employed by grade or subject teams or entire schools. A collaborative approach will make the time-saving potential even more dramatic. In addition, administrators and elementary coordinators and supervisors will find *Classroom Volunteers* to be an important source of information, as will teacher educators.

The book will also be helpful to individual volunteers and parent groups as they consider how they can make major contributions to their children's schools. Middle and high schools that are fortunate enough to have volunteers will discover that the ideas in *Classroom Volunteers* are effective for secondary schools as well.

What Is Included?

The first chapter will probably make you chuckle because it recalls some scenes that are familiar to most elementary educators. You know you should be happy when your volunteers arrive, but your response is often "Uh-oh!" This chapter will help you realize that you are not alone in these feelings and that there is definitely something you can do about it.

The next chapter will invite you to think about your volunteer program in an entirely new way from how you have probably approached it in the past. No doubt, you will be marking pages and taking notes as you consider the valuable roles that volunteers could be filling in your classroom and school.

With all of these new thoughts swirling around in your head, Chapter 3 will help you to start setting priorities and deciding which volunteer roles are most important to your situation. You will begin to establish a firm foundation for your effort.

Chapter 4 will give you concrete tips on how to recruit the kinds of helpers you have decided you would like to have. The chapter includes lots of suggestions and illustrative examples that will make "advertising" for volunteers creative and effective.

Once you have your volunteers poised for action, a key to success is taking the time to train these helpers for specialized roles. Chapter 5 will set you up for doing this effectively and efficiently. Lots of tools, such as proposed training session agendas and templates for orientation brochures, will give you a head start on this aspect of an exciting program.

There are some secrets to keeping your volunteer projects running smoothly, and Chapter 6 will reveal them. You will get a smorgasbord of ideas about how to maintain communications with your volunteers in spite of how busy you are. It will also give you tips on teaching your youngsters to work productively with helpers. Finally, the chapter will prepare you to deal with the inevitable problems that arise in any program.

Chapter 7 will provide fun for you and your volunteers as it explores ways to show your appreciation for the important helpers in your school. There are lots of practical suggestions for ongoing expressions of thanks as well as occasional special events.

Chapter 8 gives you ideas about how to reflect back on your efforts at the end of the year. It helps you identify areas of accomplishment and assists you in choosing new priorities for your volunteer program after it has been in operation for a period of time.

A special aspect of *Classroom Volunteers: Uh-Oh! or Right On!* is the wealth of Reproducible Sheets found at the end of the book. These resources will save busy educators hours, whether these materials are used as is or modified to meet the needs of particular programs.

Acknowledgments

I would like to thank Corwin Press for the delightful way in which they work with authors. They employ a perfect combination of respect for the writer along with publishing expertise that makes the challenging job of writing a pleasure. I especially thank Alice Foster for her kindness and encouragement in all of my encounters with her. And, as always, Marlene Head does a great job of orchestrating the transformation of a bundle of typed papers into a book that makes an author feel proud.

The contributions of the following reviewers are gratefully acknowledged: Dorothy A. Bauer, Gisela Ernst-Slavit, Nancy D. Tolson, and Ron Wahlen. I am grateful to my dear friend Doreen Griffin for being a dedicated and inspiring volunteer and for sharing her experiences and thoughts with me. Finally, I would like to let my husband Jerry know how much I value his enthusiasm for my writing and how much I am inspired by his talent and creativity.

About the Author

Joanne C. Wachter has been an educator for more than 20 years. She has taught in both public and private elementary schools and has 12 years of experience as a curriculum supervisor working with elementary, middle, and high school teachers. In that role, she has had the chance to visit many schools and work with teachers and administrators on issues ranging from curriculum to classroom management.

In addition to her work in education, Wachter's other love is writing. She is the author of more than 50 instructional materials and professional books for teachers. Some of her recent works, also published by Corwin Press, are *Time-Saving Tips for Teachers* (coauthored with Clare Carhart), You Don't Have to Dread Cafeteria Duty (coauthored with Dori E. Novak), and *Sweating the Small Stuff.* She also writes textbooks and uses her expertise to produce curricula, handbooks, reports, and other educational writing for school systems on a consultant basis.

Uh-Oh! 1

Here come the volunteers. This sounds like good news, but the truth is that it does not always feel like it. Have you ever been involved in one of these scenarios?

Scenario #1

You are beginning the day with your students. Everything is humming along. You have called one group to meet with you, and the rest of the children have just gotten settled into their independent activities. All of a sudden, your classroom door opens, and Mrs. Smith walks in. She announces, "I am here to volunteer. What do you want me to do?" Uh-oh!

Scenario #2

Mr. Jones has just started helping in your classroom. He told you he has experience as a volunteer, and so you set him up to assist a group with their science projects. You are busy conducting a lesson with some other youngsters. It is not very long before the children in Mr. Jones's group are running around the room, using outdoor voices, and generally behaving in a manner that is not even close to meeting your standards. Uh-oh!

Scenario #3

You have carefully explained to your volunteer, Mrs. Johnson, exactly how you need some materials prepared. Thank heavens she showed up, because you were in a real jam. You needed to have these materials ready for tomorrow. Tonight, you are expected to attend a parent-teacher event, so there will be no time to work at home. When the children have been dismissed and Mrs. Johnson has left for the day, you look at what she has done. She completely misunderstood your directions, and the materials are unusable. Uh-oh!

Scenario #4

You have an exciting social studies project ready for the children. You will be working with your youngsters on their Native American craft project. Your volunteer, Miss Lee, is going to take small groups out to make Indian pudding. The youngsters have been talking about it all morning. Just as you get them settled for the start of class, the school secretary opens your door and says, "Miss Lee just called and said she will not be able to come in today." Uh-oh!

These kinds of scenarios result in the feeling that classroom volunteers can sometimes be more of a problem than a blessing. You know you should be happy about having volunteers. It is important for parents to be involved in their children's schools. Plus, you should be able to get more done and have your work run more smoothly with volunteers, but it does not always seem to work out that way.

This situation does not have to be the case. With a carefully managed system for working with volunteers, you can turn your "uh-ohs" into "right ons."

Putting some time into planning can help your volunteer program run more efficiently and easily. Once you decide what kind of help you need, what particular volunteers can realistically contribute, and how to manage the whole situation, your volunteer program will almost run itself. The first step is thinking about volunteers in a new way.

2

Thinking About Volunteers in a New Way

Most classroom volunteer programs are time based. That is, you find out who wants to volunteer and when they can come into the classroom. This approach often ends up with you saying, "Oh, my gosh, I have recruited Mrs. Smith to work on Tuesday mornings, now what am I going to do with her?" Instead, you could approach the situation of volunteer help another way. "I need a person to.... Let's see if I can find someone to do that task." The latter approach is more likely to let you get your needs met without ending up in a panic.

What If...?

Consider starting by assessing your needs and then recruiting volunteer "staff" to meet those needs. It is ideal if you can do this thinking process during the summer months, when you have a little more time to reflect.

Specialization

A shift in thinking that is helpful with this concept is to start viewing some or all of your volunteers as specialists rather than generalists. Instead of the shotgun approach of assigning any volunteer any task that comes to mind, you can plan ahead to identify specialists who will be matched with specific needs.

The following roles are outlined to spark your thinking about the kinds of specialized volunteer staff that may be helpful to you. Start thinking about a few that might be most important to your program.

Specialized Roles for Volunteer Staff

Role
Computer Coach

Description: This role involves being on hand to work directly with children while they are using computers. The volunteer will help youngsters run their programs, solve their problems with the computer, and provide praise for good efforts and results.

Qualities Needed:
- Has used computers in his or her job or is in a computer training program in a local high school or college
- Knows the basics of computer use related to the software you use in your program
- Is able to work patiently with children

Commitment: The person would need to be available when youngsters are using computers in the classroom or a lab situation. This may be a certain time of day, such as during a Writer's Workshop, or it may involve a variable schedule. This coach's help would be especially valuable when children are first introduced to computer use or new software.

Support for Success: The volunteer would need a little orientation relative to what to expect in working with children on computers. He or she may also need to come in at a time when the software is not being used to become familiar with it.

Notes: A very dedicated volunteer with lots of time to devote could work with two or more classrooms or be stationed in a computer lab that is used by various classes.

Role
Expressive Reader

Description: This is a person who has a talent for and enjoys reading aloud to children. He or she may be called on to read to the class, small groups, or individuals.

Qualities Needed:
- Ability to read aloud fluently and expressively
- Ability to keep children engaged and focused

Commitment: The time commitment can be relatively flexible. If the Reader is a particularly strong dramatic reader, you could invite him or her to read to the entire class occasionally for a treat. In this case, you could work around the Reader's schedule. In other situations, you may seek a Reader who can commit to a certain amount of time per week to read to a small group or an individual who needs the experience of hearing someone read to motivate interest and provide a model of fluency.

Support for Success: You may furnish the Reader with some written tips for how and at what points to engage children in discussion of what is being read to them.

Notes: It is effective to set up a friendly corner with a rocker and cushions as a special place for youngsters to go to hear the volunteer read aloud to them.

Role
Writing Coach

Description: This is a helper who will meet with individual children to discuss specific pieces that the youngsters have written. The focus of the discussions is on the content and quality of the writing, not on grammar and mechanics (see Editor, p. 7).

Qualities Needed:
- Knowledge of the characteristics of good writing
- Great sensitivity to the feelings and rights of young authors

Commitment: Ideally, the Writing Coach would be available during class time allocated to writing, such as the Writer's Workshop. It may also be possible to have a Writing Coach work by pulling individuals from other activities to discuss their writing, but this situation is less desirable. Writing Coaches can work 1 or more days per week. Any time they are able to work is a plus because individual conferencing is very valuable and very labor intensive.

Support for Success: Writing Coaches require specialized training to develop the skills and sensitivity needed to be successful in this role. See Chapter 5 for specifics about this training.

Notes: A variation on the Writing Coach concept is to have a volunteer meet with peer response groups to facilitate those sessions. This practice is especially valuable when youngsters are first learning how to give peer responses. Again, the Coach should be well trained in this process.

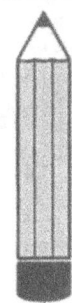

Role
Editor

Description: The Editor can work in three ways. He or she can meet with individual writers to help them peruse their work for capitalization, spelling, punctuation, and other mechanical aspects that need to be fixed before making a final copy.

Another possibility for the class Editor is to facilitate during a peer editing conference between two students. The Editor can act as a guide in helping the children find the errors that have been addressed by teacher instruction.

Finally, the Editor can be a support to you in taking a pile of papers to evaluate for mechanical errors. The Editor could be instructed to mark a few errors that need to be corrected on each paper, compliment authors on mechanics they have used well, and keep a running list of concepts that need further instruction.

Qualities Needed:
- Expertise with the mechanics of the English language
- Sensitivity to young authors

Commitment: If the Editor is going to work directly with children, he or she needs to be able to commit to some time each week when children will be involved in writing activities. If the Editor is going to help with editing papers, as described in the last option, he or she can do this task at any time and location as long as the turnaround time is reasonable.

Support for Success: If the Editor is going to work directly with children, he or she will need training in how to conduct editing conferences. See Chapter 5 on training volunteers.

Role
Reading Coach

Description: The Reading Coach will listen to individual children read. She or he will provide encouragement for using effective reading strategies and engage the child in discussion aimed at checking comprehension.

Qualities Needed:
- Willingness to be trained in the necessary skills because few will already have them

Commitment: This volunteer will have to be dedicated to regular appearance in the classroom, because only frequent practice will have an impact. The role may be shared by two individuals who can alternate and also substitute for one another when necessary.

Support for Success: Specialized training is a must. See Chapter 5 for an outline of what might be covered.

Notes: Reading Coach is one of the most demanding roles in terms of what must be learned and the commitment that should be made. On the other hand, it also has a wonderful impact on youngsters' success and thus is very rewarding.

Role
Book Discussion Facilitator

Description: This helper is a person who sits with youngsters who are discussing a book they have read. His or her job is to let the children do most of the talking and only jump into the discussion when conversation lags, when someone gets off track, or when points need clarification.

Qualities Needed:
- Enjoyment of discussing literature
- Willingness to read the book the children are discussing
- Ability to stay in the background of the discussion most of the time

Commitment: A Book Discussion Facilitator needs to be available several days a week, but only for a few weeks. Once the children have finished the particular book they are reading, the Facilitator's job is done—unless he or she wants to commit to being involved with the next book the youngsters will read.

Support for Success: The Book Discussion Facilitator will need training in how to participate in book conversations. See Chapter 5.

Role
Guest Presenter or Demonstrator

Description: This helper will have a special experience, skill, or "show and tell" to share with youngsters. The topic of the presentation or demonstration should be closely related to something the children are studying in your class.

Qualities Needed:
- Specialized expertise relative to a unit of study in your program
- Ability to hold the interest of children

Commitment: This volunteer usually makes a single appearance as opposed to being a long-term part of your program's staff.

Support for Success: Ideally, you will meet with this volunteer or at least have an extended phone conversation to go over the content of the presentation. You will be able to help him or her tailor the material to the interests of your youngsters and the objectives of your unit. You also need to provide some detailed guidance about how to keep the interest of elementary-age children.

Role
Travel Agent

Description: Your class Travel Agent will help you set up field trips. He or she can be involved in any or all of the following tasks: scouting locations, talking with representatives of the site to schedule a visit and find out any other critical information, arranging for buses, planning meal stops, determining costs and helping collect money, working on collecting permission slips from parents, and contacting and orienting chaperones.

Qualities Needed:
Your Travel Agent needs to:
- Be reliable and detail oriented
- Commit to working in advance so the arrangements are not subject to last-minute pressures

Commitment: You may have one Travel Agent that works with you on a few field trips that you plan to scatter throughout the year. On the other hand, you may use a different Travel Agent for each event.

Support for Success: Your Travel Agent will need clear directions from you at the beginning of the project. He or she will need to know any "givens," such as school policies related to field trips; procedures such as those involving parent permission; and any parameters concerning distance, costs, or meals. A great kind of support is to sit down with your Agent and make a checklist of steps that need to be taken and when each needs to be accomplished.

Role
Artist

Description: This helper is a person who can be responsible for your bulletin boards, theme decorations, posters, and other artwork that supports learning and adds to the ambiance of your classroom.

Qualities Needed:
- Artistic talent
- Ability to create quickly

Commitment: Your classroom Artist does not need to be available on a regularly scheduled basis. Rather, he or she needs to be on call for when you have a special project. Your Artist will probably be able to do a lot of his or her work at home.

Support for Success: You will want to give your Artist clear directions so that the products support learning and appeal to children at your grade level. You will also need to acquaint your Artist with the location of in-school supplies and procedures for buying additional materials when needed.

Role
Book Publisher

Description: The Book Publisher oversees a group of adults or older students who will turn your children's writing into bound books. The task involves typing and then following directions to turn materials such as cardboard, tape, and wallpaper or other interesting paper into covers.

Qualities Needed:
- Organization of people and materials
- Ability to follow directions
- Ability to work quickly

Commitment: The Book Publisher can usually set his or her own schedule in cooperation with anyone who will be working on the project.

Support for Success: The Book Publisher will need a clear set of directions. He or she will also need to be provided with materials or helped in determining how the necessary supplies might be gathered.

Role
Computer Consultant

Description: This is a helper who is willing to have you call with questions about computer capability and operation.

Qualities Needed:
- Familiarity with the kind of computers your children use
- Expertise related to the kind of computer you use for your own composing, record-keeping, and other administrative tasks
- Knowledge of computer software that might be helpful to you

Commitment: The Computer Consultant does not have to be available on a regular basis. Rather, he or she needs to agree to be on call to answer questions, troubleshoot, or make recommendations. For instance, you might call in the evening to ask advice.

Support for Success: This volunteer will be most effective if you can help him or her understand the kinds of administrative and instructional tasks involved in your program.

Role
Party Host

Description: Your Party Host will assist you in planning and implementing special events like holiday parties and author's celebrations. He or she will help you decide on decor, food, and activities. Your Host can then work on getting parents of your students to supply refreshments and also attend the event, if that would be helpful.

Qualities Needed:
- An enjoyment of parties
- Patience when faced with excited children
- Sensitivity to the importance of getting tasks done in advance

Commitment: Your Party Host will be someone you will call on periodically when you are looking forward to a special event. Much of the work can be done on his or her own schedule and at home as long as everything is ready at the appointed time.

Support for Success: Your Host will be most successful if you meet with him or her as early in the process as possible to discuss your overall vision and get additional ideas from your helper. It is also important to let the volunteer know your expectations for the children's behavior during a special event so that these can be reinforced.

Role
Secretary

Description: Your volunteer Secretary is someone who can help you with written and phone correspondence, as well as assist you in the creation of typed materials.

Qualities Needed:
- Typing skill
- Good public relations
- Ability to respond to reasonable time frames and deadlines

Commitment: Ideally, your secretary will be able to set up a regular schedule of contact with you. When he or she calls in or stops by at this appointed time every few days or every week, you will have ready a list of secretarial tasks you would like to have completed. The actual typing and phone calls can be done in your Secretary's home if that is more convenient for your helper.

Support for Success: You can assist your Secretary by being organized about the few tasks you ask him or her to do each week and by focusing on requesting that the volunteer do jobs that do not have an unreasonable deadline.

Role
Coordinator of Resources and Supplies

Description: Your Coordinator will work with you on collecting and preparing materials for special projects such as science experiments or culminating events for social studies units. In addition, or as an alternative, a Coordinator of Resources and Supplies could work with day-to-day materials. This might involve checking supplies in areas such as writing corners or art areas to be sure that all necessary materials are in adequate supply and order. If they are not, he or she may be willing to replenish them from the school supply closet or a local store if you supply the funds from your school budget.

Qualities Needed:
- Organizational skills
- Ability to anticipate needs and address them in a timely manner

Commitment: The Coordinator who works with you on special projects may need to be available only for a relatively short time before the project is scheduled to be implemented. On the other hand, a Coordinator who helps with day-to-day supplies will need to check on a regular basis to see what is needed.

Support for Success: You can support your Coordinator of Resources and Supplies by providing advance notice of your needs and by keeping a running "shopping list" of items you anticipate needing in the near future.

Role
Book Sleuth

Description: This volunteer worker helps you find books and other materials in your school media center or public library in relation to a unit or theme you are teaching. He or she does the library legwork.

Qualities Needed:
- Enjoyment of spending time in libraries
- Understanding of the level of reading materials your youngsters can read

Commitment: This volunteer needs to be called on only from time to time when you are starting something new. He or she can set a schedule as long as the materials are ready when you need them.

Support for Success: The helper will need a clear explanation from you, preferably in writing, of the topics and formats of materials you need. You may also want to show the Book Sleuth how to do a simple readability check to be sure materials are at the proper level.

Role
Internet Investigator

Description: This helper will surf the Internet for you to find and bookmark sites that relate to your units of study.

Qualities Needed:
- Skill with using the Internet
- Good judgment about which sites are appropriate for youngsters

Commitment: This volunteer should be able to work either at school or at home. He or she will need to respond to reasonable deadlines but does not have to appear in your classroom on a regular basis. An option is having several Internet Investigators who take turns surfing so that no one has to spend too much time.

Support for Success: You will help your Investigator be successful by providing detailed information about what you need and also by being sure that he or she is informed about any school or district policies about Internet use.

Role
Good Housekeeping Expert

Description: This worker is a person who enjoys bringing order to chaos. He or she comes into your room and makes it look inviting and organized after it has suffered the normal effects of a roomful of busy, active children. Your Good Housekeeping Expert may also have some ideas about how you and your youngsters can store and use materials in more efficient ways.

Qualities Needed:
- Organizational skills
- Patience for repeated tasks

Commitment: Ideally, this person will agree to come into your room on a regular basis, perhaps once a week, to put things back in their places and do general tidying up.

Support for Success: You can support your Good Housekeeping Expert by communicating with him or her about how you and your students use various materials and areas. It is also important for you to follow through in trying to implement the organizational ideas and routines being established by this helper.

Role
Interior Decorator

Description: This is a volunteer who can help you with making your classroom inviting and functional. Ask him or her for ideas about aesthetics as well as traffic flow, storage, effects of color, and ways to make the classroom feel more spacious.

Qualities Needed:
- Interior design training or a natural flair

Commitment: This volunteer is most helpful if he or she agrees to meet with you a few times during the year to evaluate your classroom and suggest ideas. It would be ideal to have a conversation with your Interior Designer as you are getting your room ready for each new school year.

Support for Success: Your Designer will need to know about your preferences and those of the youngsters you teach. He or she will also need to know about the kinds of activities conducted in your room in order to figure out what types of areas are needed.

Role
Public Relations Expert

Description: This person helps to publicize the good things your youngsters are doing. This may involve such tasks as writing articles for the school newsletter or contacting a local reporter about attending the culminating event of an interesting unit. The purpose of this publicity is to help with the goal of public support for education as well as to let your students know you recognize and appreciate their talents and efforts.

Qualities Needed:
- Knowledge of the local media or the initiative to learn
- Written and verbal communication skills
- Ability to react quickly to newsworthy events

Commitment: This volunteer needs to be willing to touch base with you regularly to find out what is newsworthy in your classroom. He or she can then write press releases or make contacts on his or her own schedule.

Support for Success: Your PR volunteer will need you to be diligent about sharing newsworthy events in a timely manner and supplying the needed information.

Role
Appreciation Coordinator

Description: This helper will assist you in keeping up with your appreciations. He or she will be sure you have materials such as note cards on hand. Your Appreciation Coordinator will collaborate with you to plan and implement big and little celebrations of special events and accomplishments in the lives of your youngsters. These functions may include activities such as establishing a program for recognizing birthdays in some simple but meaningful way or setting up a Compliment Board in the classroom or hallway to recognize thoughtful behavior and student achievements. The Appreciation Coordinator can also help you carry out the details of showing gratitude for people who do things for your class, such as a particularly good substitute or a principal who comes to a class event.

Qualities Needed:
- Sense of fun and enjoyment of celebration
- Willingness to be on the lookout for occasions for appreciation

Commitment: The Appreciation Coordinator will need to communicate with you from time to time about ideas for celebration and recognition. Most of the organizational work involved in helping you carry out the details can be done on the person's own schedule, and some of the work can probably be done at home.

Support for Success: The best way to support your Appreciation Coordinator, besides staying in contact to share information about appreciation opportunities, is to show your appreciation for him or her!

Role
Community Linker

Description: This is a person who serves as a liaison between your classroom and community organizations. He or she considers ways that community groups can support your program and how your youngsters can serve the community.

Qualities Needed:
- Creativity
- Knowledge of community organizations and their key members or the initiative and chutzpah to make contacts

Commitment: The Community Linker can be on the lookout for ideas on an ongoing basis and contact you when he or she has an idea. On the other hand, if you become aware of a program that you would like your Linker to explore, you can make the contact.

Support for Success: You can support your Community Linker by being sure he or she knows what is going on in your program so that links can be explored.

Role
Special Events and Opportunities Coordinator

Description: This person keeps his or her eyes open for special events and opportunities in the community that integrate with your program. For instance, a children's author may be coming to the community library, a special Civil War exhibit may be on display while you are doing a unit on this topic, or a television show related to your science unit may be scheduled. The Coordinator lets you know about these potential enhancements to your program.

Qualities Needed:
- Enjoyment of keeping up-to-date on what is going on in the community

Commitment: This Coordinator needs to touch base with you periodically to find out what is coming up in your program so that he or she can be on the lookout for opportunities. Your communications with this volunteer could be handled on the phone or by e-mail if in-person meetings make things more hectic for both of you.

Support for Success: To be successful, this volunteer needs you to give him or her advance notice about what your youngsters will be studying. A list of upcoming units will be especially helpful so that the Coordinator has something concrete for future reference.

Role
Donations Director

Description: The Donations Director becomes aware of the needs of your program and goes about finding innovative ways to meet some of those needs that are not included in your budget. For instance, you may want to give a book to each of your children to celebrate his or her birthday when it comes during the year, but you do not have the money. Your Donations Director may be able to find a source of free or inexpensive but nice children's books.

Qualities:
- Courage to approach people for donations
- Charm to convince them to give to your program

Commitment: The Donations Director does not need to keep a regular schedule. You can call on him or her as needed for special projects.

Support for Success: This volunteer will need to have all of the facts and figures from you so that he or she can make a convincing case for why a business or individual in the community should support your program.

It is obvious that there are many ways that volunteers can be involved in a classroom, team, or school program. There are options for people who can spend regularly scheduled time in the school, for those who might be able to help out once in a while, and those who must do volunteer work in their homes because they have full-time jobs or small children who depend on them during school hours.

What's Next?

Now that you have opened your mind to the wide range of possibilities, it is time to focus in on the particular needs in your school. Reflecting by yourself, or better yet, with your colleagues, will help you figure out what will be most helpful for your situation.

3 Setting Priorities

Your head may be swimming with possibilities at this point. As noted earlier, it is not realistic to think you can recruit people to fill all of the roles that might be helpful. You will need to set some priorities. You may want to do this individually as well as in collaboration with your colleagues. You may need to have some volunteers work exclusively in your classroom. There may be others, though, that you and one or more teachers could share, thereby spreading out the work of recruiting, training, and managing the volunteer staff's work. A collaborative approach related to at least some of the volunteer roles will keep you and all of your colleagues from going off to your separate rooms to take on the challenge of your individual volunteer programs alone. Several heads really can be better than just one!

Determining Your Biggest Needs

The following suggestions will help you and your coworkers tune in to your biggest needs and set priorities for volunteer recruiting. Use one or more of these activities to assist you in determining where you could most use help, and focus on those roles first. You can always add more later.

- Keep a Dream List journal for a few days. Leave a notebook open on your desk and put a caption on the first page, "What I could do if I had more time . . . " Every time you think of something you wish you had time to do for your students, jot down a note. Use these notes to spark ideas for what a volunteer might be able to do.

- Use a volunteer job chart to think about which are the most crucial roles for volunteers at this time. (See Reproducible 1.)
- Use a self-survey to reflect on jobs that volunteer staff could do. (See Reproducible 2.)
- Initiate an after-school or planning meeting session with some of your colleagues to brainstorm kinds of jobs for volunteers. Determine which volunteer roles might extend across classrooms or grades. For instance, a volunteer who has artistic talent might be willing to create bulletin boards for several teachers.
- Early in the year, survey parents and other potential volunteers about their talents and areas of interest. Make no commitments at this point. Simply tell the survey takers that you are assessing what expertise is available. When the surveys come in, sit down with your colleagues or alone to see which responses appeal to you the most. (See Reproducible 3.)
- Ask your administrator to consider devoting a faculty meeting to discussing options for school and classroom volunteer jobs. Use the following steps:

> *Faculty Meeting To Discuss Volunteer Program Agenda*
> - Setting the Purpose of the Meeting: To decide on priority jobs for volunteers
> - Selecting a Recorder
> - Brainstorming of Volunteer Roles
> - Voting on Priorities
> - Getting Consensus on Next Steps
> - Deciding on Date and Action Steps for Next Meeting

- Either alone or in collaboration with colleagues, create a wish list of volunteer staff and visualize what those people would do. Establish some priorities and figure out first steps. (See Reproducible 4.)

A Special Priority

A dream come true is finding someone who will act as your Chief Volunteer. Some years, you may be fortunate enough to find this kind of helper. When you do, not only will your volunteer program run more easily and efficiently, but your entire instructional program will be more effortless.

Qualities for a Good Chief Volunteer

Your Chief needs to be a person with time and enthusiasm to devote to the job because you will want someone who can stick with you through at least one school year. A good Chief is a self-starting go-getter who works well with people. It is important to find a Chief who is skilled at motivating people to be involved. Finally, it is crucial that your Chief Volunteer be someone you like, someone who is an advocate for your program, and someone with whom you can communicate easily and openly.

Responsibilities

The Chief Volunteer does not do the tasks outlined in the previous chapter. Instead, his or her main activity will relate to helping you recruit, train, coordinate, and communicate with other volunteers to your program. For instance, you can call on your Chief Volunteer to work with you to identify someone to be a volunteer Travel Agent for your upcoming field trip to a local historical site. You and the Chief could brainstorm about someone who might like to take on this task and specify the kinds of activities that would be involved. The Chief could then make some contacts and come back to you with the results.

The Chief is a communication link between you and other volunteers when things get hectic and you cannot make personal contact yourself. He or she also can serve as a sounding board for you when you need to try out an idea or develop a plan for a new aspect of your program. If you use the approach of thinking of your volunteers as specialists, a Chief can be particularly helpful in coordinating efforts and helping you keep track of projects.

Incentive for the Chief Volunteer

It is a fair question to ask why someone would want to take on the responsibilities of being an unpaid Chief in your program. Some people simply enjoy the atmosphere of a school and feel good about contributing to the worthwhile work of educators. Others see a job like this as a way to develop and gain experience with management skills that they may eventually use in a paid job when their children are older. Some already have management skills that they may not be using in a salaried position at the moment because they have elected to be a stay-at-home parent while their children are young. They might enjoy the challenge of keeping their skills current by working with you.

Whatever draws a volunteer's interest to a Chief job, you will need to do your part to be sure he or she feels appreciated enough to continue. A real plus would be an "office" in your classroom or planning room. In most schools today, space is a scarce commodity, so you will probably have to be very creative. Designating a little table or desk space for your Chief will make him or her feel a part of your program. Perhaps you could have a nameplate made to sit on the table and provide a bin of desk supplies such as pens, paper, stapler, and other frequently used items.

You might also have a nice reusable name tag with his or her name and "Chief Volunteer" printed on it. This tag can be worn by the Chief when he or she is working in the school.

In addition to being sure the Chief Volunteer has at least a little space to call home in the school, it will be extremely important to provide ongoing recognition and appreciation for this helper. There are many ideas regarding this in the chapter on appreciating your volunteers. Don't be tempted to think you cannot afford the time to carry out these ideas. If you want to enjoy the benefits of having a Chief Volunteer, you cannot afford to *not* make time to show appreciation.

What's Next?

The ideas in this section have started you thinking about volunteer priorities. The thoughts you and your colleagues have gathered by reflecting on your needs is a first step to being more deliberate in working with volunteers. Next, you will need to consider how and where you can recruit volunteers to fill your most crucial needs. The next section will help you accomplish that step.

4 Recruiting Your Volunteer Staff

You have identified possible volunteer staff roles and narrowed your wish list down to a few choices that would be most beneficial. Now, you will be faced with the challenge of finding people to fill those roles. Using the concept of volunteers as specialists, you will not want to send out a blanket request for helpers. Instead, you will want to target your recruiting efforts.

How to Invite Participation

If you decide to recruit some or all of your volunteers for specialized roles, you will need to think ahead about the specific duties and responsibilities of these helpers. First of all, you may want to list on separate pages the title of each of the volunteer roles you have decided is your priority. Use the charts in Chapter 2 as well as your own ideas (and those of other teachers if you are working collaboratively) to spell out the tasks you would like each person to perform. Think about any specialized skills they will need in order to be successful. Determine what kind of orientation or training you, your team, or school plans to offer. Finally, consider the names of anyone whom you might approach and additional places you might recruit if none of those people is interested. (The section below on "Where to Solicit Help" will be useful for this last bit of information.) Use Reproducible 5 to help organize these ideas. Remember that you should be focusing on only a few priority roles so that your volunteer program does not become overwhelming.

The information you jot down on the chart can be used to create ads, articles, or posters advertising your needs. If you make phone calls or in-person contacts, the notes can be used to help you remember all of the points you want to convey.

There are many formats and forums available for your invitations to volunteers to join your program. Some of the following may be practical for you.

Formats for Recruiting Volunteer Staff

Posters outside your classroom

Banners or announcements in the school entrance foyer

Fliers in the school office area

Personal notes sent to likely candidates for specific jobs

Phone calls to people who might be interested

Posters in community gathering places such as grocery stores and churches

Computer-made brochures to hand out at child-centered events such as Little League games, scouting events, or dance classes

Ads on the local educational television channel

Classified ad in the school newspaper

Notice to the parent-teacher organization

Letter to the parents of children in your class

Poster to hang in local senior center

Letters to professors in college education courses inviting their students to volunteer

Flier targeted to local businesses and organizations

Ads on your school's Web site

Skit or some other creative presentation during your Back-to-School Night for parents to motivate people to consider volunteering

As you draft ideas for ads or notices, begin immediately to capture the imagination of potential volunteers by highlighting the fun and rewards your volunteer staff will experience in working with you and your children. As you gather your thoughts, consider why a person would want to give up his or her time to work in your classroom or school without pay.

You need to entice people into your classroom, however, without making them feel pressured. It is true that you can lure some volunteers into your program with the guilt approach, but that is not the best choice. Attempting to push people's guilt buttons may result in some folks showing up at first, but you will not be able to rely on them for consistent, long-term support because they will be there for the wrong reason. The volunteers you want are ones who join your program because they are genuinely excited about working with you and the children.

Avoid the Guilt Approach; Try an Invitational Tone

AVOID!: If I can't get enough of you to come to our planning meetings for our Friday evening family reading night, we will have to cancel it, and the children will be horribly disappointed.

INSTEAD: Do you remember how much fun it was to snuggle up with your children and read a bedtime story to them when they were toddlers? Come help us recapture that fun for your family and others as we meet to plan our first annual family reading night. Bring your good ideas about how to make this a night to remember.

Also, consider the minimum time commitment you will need from volunteers filling particular roles. It is important to have this expectation clearly in mind and to convey it to potential volunteers immediately. You will cause frustration for yourself, your students, and the volunteer if you are not clear about what is needed. For instance, a volunteer who wants to be a Writing Coach but who can devote only an hour each month is not going to be effective. His or her energies might be channeled into another task that requires a smaller time commitment.

Consider the following examples of how to advertise for volunteers:

CALLING ALL ARTISTS!

Mr. Brown's class needs someone who likes to draw and paint to assist a small group of children in planning and making a creation for our school's Characters in Literature Door Decoration Celebration. If you can give two afternoons during the week of November 4 to this project, please contact Mr. Brown.

WANTED: READING COACHES

Come be part of the excitement of teaching youngsters to love books. Miss Smith's first-grade class needs three dedicated helpers to devote 1 hour three times a week to listening to children read. Training will be provided. Join the fun!

Where to Solicit Help

The more open-minded and creative you are about where to look for volunteer staff, the more likely you are to find just the right few helpers. An obvious place to start is by approaching parents of youngsters in your class. There are many other possibilities as well. The chart below will help you or your committee start thinking. Reproducible 6 will help you organize the contacts.

Sources of Volunteers

Parents of children in your class who wish to work in their children's rooms

Parents of children in other classes who do not wish to work in their own children's rooms but who want to help

Members of the school's parent-teacher organization

Grandparents of children who attend your school

Education majors from local colleges
High school students who are trying to earn student service hours or who have an interest in working with younger children
People from community businesses
Men and women who belong to local service groups such as Rotary Club and Lions Club
Residents of a nearby retirement home
People who frequent a neighborhood senior center
Someone who has no tie to the school or a community group who sees your poster or ad and thinks it would be fun to volunteer in a school

Not all of the people listed would be willing to volunteer on an ongoing basis. For instance, retired folks are often too delighted with their freedom to sign up for a weekly commitment, and people from local businesses are frequently tied into rigid work schedules. People from these groups and others can sometimes commit to a one-time event or short-term project. You will not know until you ask.

Security and safety are issues to keep in mind, particularly when you seek volunteers from the community at large as opposed to simply approaching adults whose children attend your school. You will need to provide some type of screening and supervision to be sure that the people you invite into your school are there for the right reasons. Some systems use fingerprinting as a partial answer to this need. Your administrator should be consulted about issues related to safety.

Figuring where to look for your volunteer staff is another perfect opportunity for collaboration. Even if you are looking for sources of volunteers to work in your room only, other teachers may be able to share success stories about creative ideas they have used for finding just the right kinds of helpers.

When to Recruit

It is a great benefit if you can begin your recruiting efforts in the summer. This approach has several advantages.

Advantages of Early Recruiting

Gives you a chance to recruit when other school demands are not competing for your attention

Allows you to know what "staff" you will have as you plan your program for the upcoming year

Makes it possible for you to train, orient, or at least begin talking with your volunteers about how you can work together before the hectic activity of the school year begins

Permits volunteers to start early in the year to support you in the extra demands of the first weeks of school

Gives your youngsters a chance to learn to work with your volunteer staff right from the beginning

Helps your volunteers feel a part of the program because they can be involved in early planning and implementation activities

As noted, there are many places you can recruit volunteers in your school, community, and beyond. Recruiting in the summer poses a particular challenge in relation to approaching parents of children in the class you will have the following fall. Many parents prefer working in their own children's classrooms, and you may not know which youngsters are assigned to your class until very late.

You and your colleagues may be able to discuss this issue with your administrator to see if there is a way you can approach potential parent volunteers for your class during the summer. Even if you will not be able to take this step, you can still talk to individuals and people from businesses and organizations outside the school. You can also recruit volunteers from the school community for tasks that will involve not just individual classrooms but grades, teams, or the school at large.

Granted, working on recruiting, planning, and orienting volunteers before the school year starts takes up some of your summer vacation. If you decide to use this approach, however, the beginning and the rest of your school year can be easier and less stressful. Plus, if you are working on some elements of your volunteer program with other teachers, the work can be divided up, and planning sessions can provide great opportunities for leisurely summer lunches with some of your favorite coworkers.

What's Next?

This section recommended that you focus your recruiting efforts around talents you need, not the times that people are available. Your next task is to consider what kinds of orientation and training activities are needed. Taking time to train helpers will make them more comfortable and will increase their effectiveness in their roles.

Training Volunteers 5

One important key to a successful volunteer program is training your "staff." It is true that when you use the specialized-role approach to building a volunteer staff, you look for people who already have skills and enthusiasm for the jobs you are asking them to do. Still, they will need at least an orientation and, in some cases, more extensive training before they are ready to be truly valuable members of your classroom program. Before you get discouraged about where you will find time to orient and train volunteers, think about how much time and stress will be saved later as a result of putting in some up-front time.

General Orientations

Chances are that many of your volunteers have not been actively involved in day-to-day elementary classroom life since they were students. Even those who have volunteered in other classrooms and become familiar with today's trends and challenges will not know your specific ways of operating. There is certain information that will be helpful to all volunteers in your classroom regardless of their specialized roles. A general orientation can provide what is needed.

Organizing an Orientation

There are several options to consider when figuring out how to structure an orientation for your volunteers. One possibility is to talk to each helper individually, one by one, and informally let him or her know the necessary information. This option, however, is labor intensive because you will be repeating the same information over and over. Additionally, the informality of the approach may fail to convey the importance of the information you need to communicate.

A more efficient alternative is to conduct a group orientation for all of those who will volunteer in your classroom. In one session, you can pass on to everyone the important information and tips for being a successful helper. You can also begin to create a sense of community among your "staff" and start to build relationships between your Chief Volunteer, if you are fortunate enough to have found one, and your specialized volunteers.

A third option is to cooperate with other teachers at your grade level or on your team to provide a collaborative orientation. A general session can be planned to convey information that is fairly standard across classrooms. There also could be a break-out time for each teacher to take his or her volunteers to the individual classrooms to share specific information. As an alternative, the break-out sessions could be organized by role rather than teacher. For example, all the volunteers who were going to act as Travel Agents could meet with one teacher, those who were going to be Good Housekeeping Experts could meet with another, and so on. There are several advantages to this collaborative approach. First, the work of organizing the orientation is spread out among several teachers so that no one has to do as much. Second, the more formal approach conveys the importance of the information. Finally, this format sets the stage for having volunteers work across two or more classrooms, if desired.

Orientation Content

The better your volunteers understand your program and what you are trying to accomplish with it, the better they will support you and fit in naturally. Some crucial information that they will need includes the following:

What All Volunteers Need to Know

Your specific expectations for children's behavior

How you will communicate with volunteers about what needs to be done and their progress in accomplishing tasks

Specifics of the tasks to be done

Where they will find materials

Location for their work

Backup plans for emergencies when they have to change their schedules

How to handle problem situations that arise while they are working with children

Naturally, as much of this information as possible will be discussed, but it is also a tremendous help to provide the information in writing. A simple volunteer handbook or even a small brochure reviewing key points will give volunteers a concrete reminder of what was presented. See Reproducible 7 for a fill-in-the-blank brochure template. Check out Reproducible 8 for possible topics to include in a volunteer handbook.

Format of the Orientation

You or you and your colleagues should use the best of what you know about instruction in planning and implementing your orientation. One aspect to consider is that your volunteers are busy people who need the necessary information presented efficiently so that they can get what they need and return to their other responsibilities for the day or evening. Providing child care may be important if some of your volunteers have toddlers or if your session is in the summer, in the evening, or on a Saturday. If you are working with colleagues, someone could be responsible for entertaining the little ones while others meet with the adults.

Another consideration is that you will be conveying a lot of new information. Just as with your young students, it is important to break up the information, provide interactive opportunities, and use visuals. In short, do not forget your good instructional practices. Not only will the information stay with participants longer, but you will provide a model of how you want the volunteers to work with your students.

Making the Orientation Special

Although your orientation is serious business in terms of the information you need to convey, it should also have an air of celebration. The first meeting with your volunteers is an excellent opportunity to start letting them know how much you appreciate their dedication and enthusiasm for the tasks they have agreed to undertake.

Attending to details such as having refreshments and meeting in a location in the school that you have adorned with simple decorations such as flowers and balloons can set the tone for a good year. You might also want to create a letter of appreciation for your principal to sign individually for each volunteer who completes the orientation.

Eastcliff Elementary
61 Eastcliff Drive
Baltimore, Maryland 22190

Dear Mrs. Evans,

Thank you for taking time to attend our Volunteer Orientation. We appreciate your willingness to be part of our program and are impressed with your commitment to the education of young children. We look forward to an exciting year. With your help, our youngsters will be able to do more than ever before. Please let me know how I can assist you in feeling comfortable at Eastcliff.

Sincerely,

Dr. Jerry Michaels
Principal

Your general orientation will take a little planning and time, but it can be an enjoyable and beneficial event for both you and your volunteers. The effort you put into this occasion will result in a more efficient and dedicated staff of volunteers to make the school year easier for you and more profitable for your children.

Specialized Training

Considering that the concept of specialization is an important part of the approach in *Classroom Volunteers*, each of your volunteers is going to need support relative to his or her area of concentration. Many of these roles, however, can be handled with on-the-job training once the volunteer has completed the general orientation. Some jobs, however, will require more in-depth training. If you have identified one or more of these roles as your priorities for this year, you will have to consider how and when to provide the necessary training. Once again, you are encouraged to consider collaborating with your colleagues to deliver these workshops in an efficient, enjoyable way.

Which Roles

The roles that are "musts" for additional training are those that involve very specialized interactions with children. It is your responsibility as the caretaker of not only your students' academic progress but their self-esteem to ensure that your volunteers are skilled at knowing how to communicate with children in a positive, growth-producing way. These considerations are especially crucial in the following roles:

Roles for Specialized Training
Expressive Reader
Writing Coach
Editor
Reading Coach

Nature of the Training

This training should be carefully planned using the principles of good instruction and honoring the needs of adult learners. In the case of specialized training, even more than the general orientation, working with other teachers to deliver the training makes sense. For example, there is no reason the school cannot offer a session to prepare Editors across grade levels. The presenters can show participants examples of what to expect from young authors of various ages.

Specialized training sessions should include opportunities to see demonstrations of the skills being learned, such as how to conduct a conference with a young writer, as well as chances for guided practice. If you do some training in the summer, you may have to forgo these aspects until school is in session, but it is still a valuable piece of advice.

See Reproducibles 9 through 13 for outlines of what you may want to include in each type of training. Of course, you will need to modify these to fit your own needs and the expertise of your volunteers, but they will provide a starting point.

A Special Opportunity

Many of today's schools have the benefit of including families from various cultures and backgrounds. These parents can be called on to share their culture as part of social studies units and other special events. It is important, however, to be sure that parents of diverse backgrounds also feel welcome and successful in other types of volunteer efforts.

A bit of additional training and support may be needed if particular volunteers are from cultures where schools operate differently from those in the United States. Also, if language is a factor, the parent may need to start with tasks that are not heavily language dependent or work with a partner to get used to your school's customs as well as to have support with English. Not only can volunteers from diverse cultures enrich your program, but they can also meet other parents and become acclimated to the community. Check with your district's ESL coordinator to get additional ideas about involving multicultural volunteers.

Making the Training a Festive Event

As suggested for the general orientation, providing an atmosphere of celebration will help your participants know that they are appreciated for their efforts. Some fun touches like snacks, awards, and possibly door prizes will make learning more enjoyable. You might also invite a "dignitary," such as the principal or a central office representative, to kick off the workshop with a few words of appreciation for the important jobs that the volunteers are learning to do.

The endpoint of your seminar is another opportunity for recognition and celebration. This may be the time for a special treat. You might honor the participants' work with a little graduation ceremony, including certificates of completion of training to be handed out by your administrator.

For these more complex and specialized jobs, you might want to consider having a few reunion and refresher events during the school year to allow those who have been trained to get together to share successes, ask questions, and learn a little more about their specialized roles.

Coaching for Presenters and Demonstrators

Presenters and demonstrators usually are scheduled for one-time events in your classroom. It is still important to be sure that things will run smoothly. Even seasoned presenters will benefit from some tips about how to appeal to your particular class and how to integrate their material with your curriculum.

Consider which of the following reminders might be helpful to each of the guest presenters you might invite into your classroom:

Tips for Presenting to Children

Do's	Don'ts
Be very well prepared	Try to ad lib the majority of your comments
Speak with excitement and enthusiasm for your topic	Present dry facts or talk in a monotone
Keep your presentation to a reasonable length	Present a lengthy dissertation on your topic no matter how interesting it is
Consider breaking up your presentation with some involvement activities, but get suggestions for how to keep interaction under control	Lecture

Providing tips often can be done in a phone conversation or a short meeting. This interaction should take place well in advance of the scheduled visit, as opposed to on the day of the event, so that the guest has adequate time to think about how to incorporate the tips into the presentation.

What's Next?

It is obvious that the training component of your volunteer program will require planning and effort on your part. Because of this fact, you are again encouraged to think in terms of recruiting a small number of volunteers to do a few of the most important jobs. You can always add more roles later, but it is better to train a few people well than to overextend yourself. Keep in mind that your goal is to make your job with volunteer staff easier, not more challenging.

Maintaining a Smoothly Running Program 6

Setting up your volunteer program carefully is an important key to success. Just as critical is building in elements that will keep your program in good shape. These components involve being sure that your children know how to work with volunteer staff, setting up mechanisms for communicating with your volunteers, and handling problems effectively.

Teaching Your Children About Working With Volunteers

A volunteer should be respected by your youngsters as another teacher. Volunteer staff should also be treated as honored guests because they are donating their time. You need to set the tone for the students to take your volunteer staff seriously. This step will ensure that the children get the most out of the experience and that the helpers want to come back.

What Your Children Need to Know About Volunteers

Children need to interact with volunteers by employing common courtesy and appreciation. Common courtesy is not, however, so common until it is explicitly taught to young people. There are certain behaviors and ways of interacting that need to be clarified for your children in order to achieve success in working with volunteer staff. Some of the behaviors your youngsters need to know are the following:

Behaviors That Children Need to Learn to Work Successfully With Volunteers

Volunteer staff are to be treated with the same respect as any other adult who works in the school.

Youngsters are to follow the same rules and expectations for routines and behaviors when they work with volunteers as when they work with you.

Time spent with Writing Coaches, Expressive Readers, and other specialized volunteers can be fun, but it is work time, not play time.

Children need to have effective ideas about how to handle any problems or concerns that arise related to working with the volunteer staff.

How Children Learn These Behaviors

It does not work to assume that children know how to behave and work with volunteers. You cannot take for granted that they will spontaneously transfer their good habits in working with you to working with another adult. Youngsters need input, guided practice, and feedback to learn these skills.

Mini-lessons, role-playing, and simple games can be used to teach important behaviors. (See Reproducible 14 for some ideas.)

Keeping Track of Progress

Self-evaluation and teacher feedback will help youngsters keep the focus on skills needed for successful work with volunteers. Evaluation, no matter how informal, will also help youngsters move to independence in these behavior skills you are attempting to teach.

You can use a simple self-evaluation form for a few moments after a volunteer has finished working in your room for the day. The format could be as simple as the one on Reproducible 15. Because you will not want this activity to take up much of your precious instructional time, you might make up a simple form and have a pile of copies available to use whenever you wish. As an alternative, you might have a class chart that hangs in your room for ready access in spare moments when you want to call attention to skills used in working with volunteer staff. An overhead that you can erase and use repeatedly will also work.

Keeping the Lines of Communication Open

Consider how hard it is to keep track of your children's progress when they are working with you. It stands to reason that it is even more challenging to keep up-to-date on what is happening with your youngsters when they work with volunteer staff. If you plan ahead, however, you can make these communications deliberate, efficient, and manageable.

Format of Communications

It is not usually realistic to make teacher-volunteer communications dependent on meetings or phone calls. Both of you are too busy to fit more meetings onto your already packed calendars. It is more efficient to use paper-and-pencil formats to keep in touch with your volunteers whenever possible. When either of you has a question about these written notes, you can always follow up with personal contact.

Communication Tools

You need to have two kinds of correspondence with your volunteer staff. First, you must be able to convey tasks and directions to them. Just as importantly, they need to be able to furnish feedback about progress being made on these tasks.

If you are using the approach of specialized volunteer staff, you can create simple task and response forms for each specialist. Both types of communication can be combined on one sheet, if you wish. See Reproducibles 16 through 21 for examples.

Your communication sheets should provide specific information in a way that communicates at a glance. Your volunteer has enough to do without reading paragraphs of directions or writing lengthy responses; you have enough to do without creating or reading pages of communications, too. Check Reproducibles 22 and 23 for some other communication forms that may be helpful for various aspects of your volunteer program.

Handling Problems

Even when you and your volunteers have the best intentions and think you have set up a successful volunteer program, problems can arise. It is a natural part of any complex project. Bumps in the road do not necessarily have to lead to distress. They can lead to learning better ways of implementing programs and communicating about them. This section will help you troubleshoot various kinds of challenges that surface frequently in volunteer programs.

Preventing Problems

The idea behind *Classroom Volunteers* is to set up a solid program that avoids problems. The concepts of carefully considering your options, selecting specialized staff for your most important needs, providing training, and keeping the lines of communication open are all aimed at an easy-to-manage, (almost) problem-free volunteer program.

An important tip for preventing problems is to avoid backing yourself into a corner from the start. That is, be honest with volunteers about the fact that you are trying a new model for volunteerism in your school or classroom. Let them know that you do not have all the answers and will probably need to make changes along the way. Assure them that you will seek and value their input as the year progresses. This approach will make it easier for you to revise your course if a particular person is not working out in a particular role. You will be able to say more easily that you would like the option of using his or her talents in a different manner or would like to restructure the role in some way. This practice allows you wiggle room while still being sensitive to a person who is trying his or her best to be helpful.

Knowing When You Have a Problem

How do you know when something is wrong with your volunteer program? This may seem like a silly question, but it is probably one of the most important ones. The faster and better you are at being a problem detector, the more likely it is that your problems will be small ones that you can handle easily. It is the festering problems that can be most disruptive and hard to solve.

Notice your feelings in relation to your volunteers and volunteer program. If you find yourself feeling relaxed and confident, you probably do not have any problems in the wings at this point. As soon as you start to feel the least bit uneasy, however, take note. If you are starting to grumble that the program is causing more work, or if you are worried that your children may not be getting the experience you intended, it is time to slow down and sniff out the source of your discomfort. Maybe it is one of the problems addressed in the following charts.

Try This

Problem: What if my volunteer does not show up on time?

Example: You may have asked your Reading Coach, Mr. Brown, to appear at the beginning of reading time. He is repeatedly showing up 15 minutes after the language arts block starts and disturbing the flow of your class.

Try This: Talk directly to Mr. Brown without beating around the bush. Say something like, "I envisioned having you with us at the start of reading period, but I see that that is not working out for you. My need is to be able to continue working with the children once I start a reading group. What will work for you?" Mr. Brown might realize the reason for your request and be able to meet it.

On the other hand, he may have other responsibilities that make arriving at the time you request impossible. You might negotiate a new plan, such as leaving written directions so that you do not have to stop your group, or asking this Coach to come later when you have a break between groups. You can agree to try a particular solution for a given period of time and see if it is working for both of you.

Problem: *What do I do if my volunteer repeatedly fails to show up?*

Example: Mrs. Mack has agreed to stop by each Friday morning to pick up notes about a few secretarial tasks you would like to have done. She comes through about 50% of the time. Otherwise, this helper may show up on a different day or not at all. You never can predict.

Try This: Explain to Mrs. Mack (again) why a regular schedule is important to you in terms of having materials ready and in being able to count on certain tasks being done. Ask if there is some other regular schedule that would work better. If so, try it.

Another alternative is to see if the Secretary would prefer to communicate by phone or e-mail. Try this. If you cannot come to a workable schedule, begin looking for another volunteer Secretary. When you find one, tell Mrs. Mack that Miss White has said she would like to do secretarial work, too, and will be coming in every Friday. You can then save some jobs for Mrs. Mack that are things that would be nice to have done but are not essential to your peace of mind.

Problem: *What if my volunteer does not meet deadlines?*

Example: You are planning a great science unit about things that sink and float. Mr. Berger, your Coordinator of Resources and Supplies, has agreed to collect some items for science learning centers that you want to start on Monday. You had asked Mr. Berger to have these items to you the week before so that you could be sure everything was ready. You have not heard from him, so you call his house on Friday before leaving school. His wife answers and says he has just left for a business trip and will not be back until next Wednesday.

Try This: There is nothing you can do about Monday's project except spend part of your weekend getting the materials. However, when Mr. Berger returns on Wednesday, call and speak with him about the problem. "Mr. Berger, I am afraid we had some miscommunication. It was my understanding that you were going to have materials to me by Friday. I ended up having to gather them over the weekend. What happened?"

Mr. Berger may say that he is sorry but that the conversation you had with him about this totally slipped his mind. He seems genuinely distressed.

You may want to give Mr. Berger some extra support in meeting your deadlines, such as writing down what you need and checking in with him a little earlier. If unmet deadlines prove to be a pattern, however, it may be causing more trouble than it is worth. You may want to phase out Mr. Berger's services and look for a more deadline-conscious Coordinator.

***Problem:** What if the children disregard my behavior expectations when they are working with a certain volunteer?*

Example: Janie Sims goes to the high school that is next to your elementary. She hopes to be a teacher, so she jumped at the chance to use her free period to walk across to your room and serve as a Book Discussion Facilitator. Janie did a great job during the training workshop your team offered, and she seemed ready to take on the job. Very quickly, however, you noticed that the children were joking, shoving, and generally off task when they met with her to discuss their books.

Try This: Janie is probably as uncomfortable as you are with this situation. She wants to be successful, too. Maybe you threw her into the situation too fast. Ask her to sit with you as you meet with a group. Invite her to take notes on techniques you use to get the children to stay on task. Conduct a follow-up discussion with her about what she notices. Slowly wean her into taking over the group.

Also, remember the importance of mini-lessons for your students on how to work with a volunteer. Help Janie conduct a discussion at the end of her book groups about what positive behaviors the children feel they exhibited and where they need to improve.

Problem: What if my volunteer is teaching in a way that is contrary to my program?

Example: You notice that one of your Editors, Mr. Grayson, is using a red pen to mark every error on a child's paper. You believe that this is demoralizing to a young writer, and that only a few areas for improvement should be noted on each page.

Try This: Tell Mr. Grayson that you appreciate how seriously he is taking the role of Editor. Genuinely compliment him on his knowledge of grammar and usage. Tell him you would like to mention one thing you have noticed about young authors . . . that they respond well to concentrating on a few kinds of errors at a time. Offer him an article that explains this point of view.

Tell him you do not want to miss the good information he has been noticing about the entire spectrum of errors he is seeing, and suggest that it would be helpful if he would keep a running list so that you can address these issues in class lessons.

Problem: What if a volunteer is not keeping confidential information to himself or herself?

Example: You were delighted when Clara James offered to be your Computer Coach. She faithfully shows up each time your youngsters are scheduled for the computer lab and does a lovely job of helping when they experience computer glitches as they use the reading program you have been assigning for the slower developing readers. Everything felt like it was going fine until the woman that lives next door to you said, "I don't know if I should say anything about this, but last night at my party, Clara was going on about how hopelessly slow your student Sally Smith is."

Try This: You need to directly approach Mrs. James with this serious concern without turning off this valuable volunteer. Start into the conversation with a preamble, and do everything you can think of to try to guard her dignity, because she is a good volunteer.

"Mrs. James, I feel awkward talking to you about this because I am sure you did not realize it could cause a problem. Someone said they overheard you talking about one of the students in my class. It is kind of second nature to teachers not to talk about their students outside the school, but I know that confidentiality concerns might not be so obvious to others. I very much appreciate and rely on your help, so I do not mean to be critical, but I need to ask you to avoid talking about any of the kids outside of school. I know you will understand."

Problem: *What if a volunteer is unkind or impatient with your students?*

Example: One of your youngsters has come to you in tears. He said Mr. Evans, the Writing Coach, was sitting in on a peer conference. When this youngster read his first draft, Mr. Evans said, "Well, that sounds like something a kindergartener would write!" You have this sinking feeling that the report is accurate because another child did not seem quite himself after Mr. Evans met with him last week, but she would not tell you what was wrong.

Try This: This is a problem that cannot be tolerated. You need to confront Mr. Evans directly with what you have heard. You need to tell him that whether this is what he actually said or not is not important; your concern is the fact that the child perceived that his writing was being put down. You can try to explain the delicate nature of the young writer and how easily it can be damaged. Mr. Evans may see your point. It is more likely that, if sarcasm is his nature, you will lose him as a volunteer . . . and that is the good news, because you cannot afford to have anyone approach your children with anything short of tenderness and compassion.

Problem: What if a volunteer is not following your directions?

Example: Dr. Grant has an excellent reading voice, and you have asked her to be an Expressive Reader for your class once a month. You talked with her about stopping occasionally to get children's reactions as she read and also engaging them in a bit of discussion at the end of the reading. However, she has been interrupting her reading with a string of insignificant questions that bore children and get them off track. Then, she ruins the end of the story by quizzing them when she finishes reading.

Try This: It is important to remember that most adults' last up-close and personal experience with school was when they were students. You often have to show as well as tell volunteers what you expect. Tell Dr. Grant what a beautiful job of reading she does, and suggest that the children are so eager to hear her rendition of stories that they do not want much discussion during the story. Give her some examples of the kind of questions that might engage them. Perhaps, one day when she is coming in, you could arrange to be just finishing a reading of your own and model the kind of discussion you prefer.

What If I Am Still Uncomfortable?

You may catch on quickly that you are feeling uncomfortable about something, try one of the ideas in the Try This charts or one of your own ideas, and still not feel satisfied. Do not settle for this situation. Continue to seek a solution so that you can feel enthusiastic about all of your volunteer staff and their work.

This is another excellent opportunity to mention the positive impact of collaboration. No doubt some of your colleagues have experienced the same challenge that is facing you . . . with the same type of volunteer . . . maybe with the exact same volunteer! Brainstorm with one of the other teachers about solutions. Even better, if you are using the idea of collaborating with coworkers for planning, training, and other aspects of a school or team volunteer program, why not have regularly scheduled, brief check-up meetings to share successful ideas and brainstorm solutions to nagging problems?

What's Next?

In addition to being sure that your program runs smoothly, there is another important step that will keep volunteers coming back to your classroom. That step is showing your appreciation. This aspect of a volunteer program can be fun for you, your children, and of course, your helpers.

7 Showing Appreciation for Volunteers

Volunteering can be a thankless job. Do not let it be ... or you will soon find yourself without a volunteer program. It is rather spectacular to think that someone is willing to find time in a busy life to work for you without pay. Realize that the motivation for many school volunteers is simply to contribute to the life of their children and the lives of other youngsters. That attitude deserves appreciation, and you can have fun showing your gratitude.

Ongoing Ways of Saying "Thanks"

First of all, be assured that you do not have to spend big money out of your own wallet to express your appreciation of volunteers to your classroom, team, or school. There are many simple, inexpensive, quick ways to say, "I appreciate what you do." Some of the things you can do are the following:

Ways of Saying Thank You

Send a thank-you note to a volunteer staff member.
Make a computer-generated appreciation banner and hang it in the foyer or outside your classroom to surprise your volunteers.

Write a press release to your local paper about something a volunteer has accomplished with your children.

Stop by the florist and get a single rose for a volunteer who has done something special.

Next time you buy or bake a treat for your family, bring a piece to a volunteer staff member.

Ask the principal to write a note of appreciation or stop by to express gratitude to a volunteer for a particular contribution.

Keep a disposable camera on hand and take photos of your volunteers working with children. Give your helpers copies to take home.

Make an Attitude of Gratitude bulletin board or poster and join your students in jotting down their thank-yous for specific things volunteers have done.

You can also be on the lookout for volunteer awards and certificates. Some state government agencies of volunteerism or state departments of education have volunteer award programs. Another important aspect of showing appreciation and building team spirit among your volunteer staff is to invite them to special events and milestone markers in your program. Be sure they receive invitations to parties, fun culminating events for units, and end-of-year celebrations. After all, your volunteer staff is part of your class family for the year, and they should be included in "family" events.

Celebrations

From time to time, you might want to spice up the ongoing appreciations with special celebrations. Most likely, you will undertake these bigger thank-yous in collaboration with your school or at least your team. For example, you might want to put together a luncheon, reception, or even a potluck dinner for your volunteer staff members. There are lots of ways you can make this kind of event memorable for your helpers. Consider an agenda such as the following:

Volunteer Celebration Luncheon

Welcome by Principal Jane Lee

Poem "We Love Our Volunteers" by Jamie Dunn, 4th grade

Luncheon

Introduction of Guest Speaker

What a Volunteer Means to a School
Pete Levin, Central Office Supervisor

Awarding of Certificates

Musical Selections by 5th-Grade Chorus

Final Remarks by Principal

Some other ways you can put fun, excitement, and of course, gratitude into your event are the following:

Ways to Make Your Event Memorable

Have placemats made by the children.

Invite school or community "celebrities" to be part of your volunteer celebration.

Award door prizes.

Give each volunteer a little book or a picture made by a child.

Include a slide show of scenes showing volunteers working with youngsters in your school.

Give each volunteer a badge or button made especially for him or her.

Have children serve meals or snacks to the volunteers.

Identify someone to share real-life success stories about activities of particular volunteers in the program.

Even though it takes some work to create special celebrations for your volunteers, it is worthwhile. After all, think of how many hours dedicated, effective volunteers save you.

The Best Thank-Yous

The signs of appreciation that seem to mean the most to volunteers are those that come from the youngsters. This fact makes sense because school volunteers are usually motivated by a fondness for youngsters and a belief in the importance of their educational success. Volunteers treasure notes, pictures, and cards from the children. It is important that these simple ways of recognizing and honoring the contributions of volunteers are sprinkled throughout the school year, not just heaped on volunteers in June. Little signs of appreciation for their impact can keep them motivated to continue their roles.

What's Next?

Appreciations and celebrations provide fun memories to look back on in relation to your volunteer program. There is another kind of looking back that is beneficial to your efforts as well. Taking the time periodically to reflect on how your program is going and how you can make it even more enjoyable and beneficial is a good idea. The next chapter will help you start thinking about how you can do this.

8 Deciding Where to Go From Here

At the end of each school year, or even more often, it is important to reflect on your volunteer program and see what is pleasing you and what you might to do differently in the future. There are several lenses through which you can examine your program.

Examining Your Program

See how you are feeling about various aspects of your program. Find out how your volunteer staff is feeling about the program, and collect their good ideas for modifications that will make things run even more smoothly. Finally, invite input from your youngsters.

Your Reflections

Teachers have a tendency to continually monitor and assess how their classrooms are operating, so in a sense, evaluation of your volunteer efforts is ongoing. It is also valuable to treat yourself to a little focused reflection time concerning your program accomplishments. Why not schedule 15 minutes to sit down in a comfortable spot with a cup of coffee and consider questions such as those on the chart on the next page? To make the most of your time, you might want to jot down your thoughts so that you don't forget any of your ideas.

Reflection Questions

1. When you think of your volunteer program, what kinds of feelings do you experience? Why do you think that is the case?
2. Which of your volunteers are working out very well? What is so effective about how they do their jobs?
3. Which of your volunteers might need some further direction or need to be channeled into another role? How could you accomplish that?
4. How do you think your volunteers are feeling about working with you? Why?
5. How do you think your children view your volunteer staff?
6. Are there any volunteer roles you used this year that you may not want to continue using next year?
7. Are there any roles that you feel are important to add next year? What will you have to do to prepare for those additions?
8. Are there any colleagues that you want to ask for ideas about particular aspects of your volunteer program? What are the specifics?
9. What else is important about how your volunteer program has worked this year?

If you have been working collaboratively with other teachers on a volunteer program, you might want to have a group evaluation after you give yourself time for a personal assessment. This session is a great excuse for a little end-of-the-year celebration of your successes.

Ideas From Your "Staff"

Your thoughts provide a crucial aspect of program evaluation. It is equally important that you collect observations and suggestions from the volunteer staff that has worked with you this year. You need to hear what your workers feel are the strengths and areas for future growth of your program.

You can make this evaluation part of an end-of-the-year celebration that brings together all of your helpers. You might provide time for group brainstorming as well as a process for individualized input. For the latter, a survey such as the one on Reproducible 24 would be helpful in collecting this information.

Input From the Children

When you are evaluating your volunteer efforts, do not forget to communicate with your children about this aspect of your instructional program. Youngsters will have a different perspective and may be able to point out some details that you had not noticed. They may also have worthwhile ideas about additional ways that volunteers can work with them and you on activities and to ease the workload on you.

A survey like the one on Reproducible 25 may be useful in gathering your children's ideas. If you work with primary youngsters, a discussion may be more efficient. Because your youngsters will have experienced so much by the end of the school year, it is a good idea to reminisce with them about which people have served as helpers and what they have done so that the children recall a broad range of volunteer roles, not just recent or ongoing activities.

Creating the Next Stage of Your Vision

After you have collected your own thoughts and those of volunteers and children, it is time to sketch out your action plan for next year. This step does not have to involve a lot of formality. Simply jot down alone, or with colleagues if you are working collaboratively, your goals for the program. Picture how you would like the program to run in the future. Many aspects will duplicate the good things that have happened already.

Very likely, you will also have some dreams of changes or additions you would like to implement. Be sure you are focusing on priorities and being realistic as you fine-tune your vision. Remember that your volunteer program should be designed to make teaching easier and more pleasant, not more complicated and frustrating.

Making Good Use of the Time You Are Saving

As you reflect back on the benefits of your volunteer program and look ahead to innovations for the future, remember why you considered using helpers in the first place. You wanted to provide more quality time with your students by having some of the routine tasks handled so that you could focus more directly on the high-quality activities such as small groups and one-to-one attention and instruction.

You also wanted to stop working so hard. As a dedicated educator, you probably would not want to admit this out loud... so there, it is stated for you. There is nothing wrong with dreaming of having more time for yourself, your family, and friends. These are very important aspects of life, and you deserve to participate in them to the fullest extent possible.

Therefore, the question is, "Are you preserving and using the time that volunteers can save you to enjoy your students, family, and friends more?" It is hoped that you are not filling this gift of time with more frantic busy work. If so, one of your priority goals for your volunteer program next year should be to be more discriminating about recognizing how your volunteer program can give you the gift of extra time, and then commit to using that time wisely. Write this vision down as a promise to yourself right now, and prepare to enjoy the results.

Reproducible Sheets

REPRODUCIBLE 1

Brainstorming Jobs for Volunteers

Tasks you don't like to do, but someone else may not mind doing	Clerical tasks or administrivia that take you away from quality time with your students

Joanne C. Wachter, *Classroom Volunteers: Uh-Oh! or Right On!* Copyright © 1999, Corwin Press, Inc.

REPRODUCIBLE 2

Self-Survey: Setting Priorities

List some roles that interest you.

Rate the roles.

Roles	How did I ever live without this kind of help?	It would be nice if . . .	Somewhat useful but not that important

Joanne C. Wachter, *Classroom Volunteers: Uh-Oh! or Right On!* Copyright © 1999, Corwin Press, Inc.

REPRODUCIBLE 3

Survey Form for Potential Volunteers

Dear Families:

As we plan our volunteer program for the year, we are curious about the kinds of interests and talents that might be available. We would appreciate it if you would take a few moments to jot down answers to the following:

What hobbies, collections, or other interests might you be willing to share with our youngsters if they fit in with our curriculum?

Have you taken trips to areas of our country or other countries that might be covered in our curriculum?

Do you have a special interest in sharing your talents in any of the following areas?

- ____ Computers
- ____ Editing
- ____ Planning parties and other special events
- ____ Secretarial skills
- ____ Reading aloud
- ____ Planning field trips
- ____ Other

What other volunteer expertise might you be willing and able to offer?

Parent's Signature _____   Date _____

Joanne C. Wachter, *Classroom Volunteers: Uh-Oh! or Right On!* Copyright © 1999, Corwin Press, Inc.

REPRODUCIBLE 4

Wish List of Volunteer Staff

List the volunteer "staff" members you would like to have.	*Visualize and describe that person's talents and qualities.*	*Mark your three top priorities.*	*Next to the spaces you marked as priorities, note which first steps you would have to do to make your wish come true.*

Joanne C. Wachter, *Classroom Volunteers: Uh-Oh! or Right On!* Copyright © 1999, Corwin Press, Inc.

REPRODUCIBLE 5

Role: _____

Tasks the person will do:	
Skills the volunteer will need:	Orientation/training you can provide:

REPRODUCIBLE 6

Sources of Volunteers

Source	To be checked?	Contact information	Person who will contact
Parents of children in my class	YES NO		
Parents of children in other classes	YES NO		
Parent-teacher organization	YES NO		
Grandparents of children in my class	YES NO		
Education majors from local college	YES NO		
High school students	YES NO		
Retirement home	YES NO		
Senior center	YES NO		
Local business _____	YES NO		
Local business _____	YES NO		
Organization _____	YES NO		
Organization _____	YES NO		
Service organization _____	YES NO		
Other _____	YES NO		

Joanne C. Wachter, *Classroom Volunteers: Uh-Oh! or Right On!* Copyright © 1999, Corwin Press, Inc.

REPRODUCIBLE 7a

Orientation Brochure Template

Outside

Your Important Job as Part of Our Volunteer Staff	Where You Can Find Supplies	Some Special Tips for Volunteers

Joanne C. Wachter, *Classroom Volunteers: Uh-Oh! or Right On!* Copyright © 1999, Corwin Press, Inc.

REPRODUCIBLE 7b

Orientation Brochure Template

Inside

An Overview of the Job That We Need You to Do	How You Can Expect Children to Work With You	How You and I Can Communicate

Joanne C. Wachter, *Classroom Volunteers: Uh-Oh! or Right On!* Copyright © 1999, Corwin Press, Inc.

REPRODUCIBLE 8

Sample Table of Contents for Volunteer Handbook

1. Welcome to Our Program

2. Purposes of Our Volunteer Program

3. Types of Volunteer Jobs

4. Training for Roles

5. Negotiating a Schedule You Can Live With

6. Gaining the Attention and Cooperation of Children

7. Communicating With Teachers

8. Matters of Confidentiality and Other Important Issues

9. How to Handle Problems

REPRODUCIBLE 9

Planning Frame for Training Expressive Readers

Warm-Up

- Welcome participants.
- Invite them to share good childhood memories of having parents, siblings, librarians, or others read to them.

What Skills Participants Will Learn

- Selecting a story for reading aloud
- Reviewing and planning the reading of the story
- Using your voice to create interest and enhance comprehension
- Employing effective strategies to keep children's attention

Tips for Reading Expressively

Outline steps such as the following for participants:

- Pick a story that you love and think that children will love too.
- Read through the story initially to yourself to get the meaning.
- Reread the story to determine how you can use changes in voice, pace, volume, and body language.
- Find one or two places where you might want to stop for predictions.
- Think about how to invite sharing of feelings or other discussion when the story is finished.

Other Tips for Keeping the Attention of Children

Point out these and any other tips that will help readers:

- Be sure the length of the story matches the attention span of the audience.
- Select a story that has engaging pictures.
- Sit more restless children near you.
- Show your excitement.

Joanne C. Wachter, *Classroom Volunteers: Uh-Oh! or Right On!* Copyright © 1999, Corwin Press, Inc.

REPRODUCIBLE 9 (continued)

- Do not start until everyone is comfortable and settled.
- In a caring and sensitive way, ask anyone who is restless to move to a less distracting place.

Demonstration of Effective Expressive Reading

- Have volunteers visit a classroom or view a tape that shows how a story can be read effectively.

Discussion of Why the Demonstration Was Effective

- After the demonstration, have the participants verbalize what they saw that relates to the information you shared, as well as other strategies that might have been used.

Selection of a Short Piece to Read Expressively

- Help each participant to select a short story to use with a group of children.

Partner Practice

- Let participants select partners with whom to practice reading their stories.

Opportunity to Read to Small Group With Peer Feedback

- Set up a chance for participants to practice reading aloud to a small group of children. Let partners observe each other and note effective practices.

Group Discussion of What They Learned During the Practice Opportunity

- Give the group a chance to share their experiences with their practice.

Questions and Answers

- Let participants ask any questions they have at this point.

Note: An alternative to having you and your colleagues deliver this workshop is to see if your media specialist or public librarian might be able to offer the workshop based on his or her training.

Joanne C. Wachter, *Classroom Volunteers: Uh-Oh! or Right On!* Copyright © 1999, Corwin Press, Inc.

REPRODUCIBLE 10

Planning Frame for Training Writing Coaches

Warm-Up

- Welcome participants.
- Encourage volunteers to imagine that you asked them to share a piece of writing with the group for their critique. Have them identify specific fears they might have about doing this.

Explanation of Which Skills Will Be Addressed

- Differentiating between writing and editing skills
- Identifying several positive comments to make to each author
- Planning two or three focus points to discuss with an author
- Determining how to discuss these focus points with the author
- Honoring the author's right to make final decisions

Observation of Teacher Coaching Young Writer

- Arrange to have volunteer coaches watch live or videotaped teacher coaching sessions with one or more young authors.

Listing by Participants of Effective Techniques They Observed

- Engage the volunteers in a discussion of effective techniques they observed. List these on a chart.

Discussion by Presenter of Additional Tips

Point out any additional tips that the observers did not notice or that were not employed during this session. These may include the following:

- Find several points on which you can genuinely compliment the writer.
- Focus on just a couple of coaching points rather than overwhelming the child.

Joanne C. Wachter, *Classroom Volunteers: Uh-Oh! or Right On!* Copyright © 1999, Corwin Press, Inc.

REPRODUCIBLE 10 (continued)

- Ask questions to inspire the child to think about his or her piece rather than telling the child how to change the writing.
- Avoid taking the paper out of the child's possession. Let the author hold onto the paper and make any changes or notes on it.
- Let the child make the final decision about which changes to implement.

Opportunity to Plan a Coaching Session for a Child

- Distribute a piece of children's writing to each participant. Ask volunteers to work in pairs to find several compliments to make on each paper. Have each identify one teaching point and plan how to discuss that point with the author.

Implementing the Coaching Plan

- Provide an opportunity for the pairs of coaches to meet with the authors of their papers and implement their plans.

Peer and Presenter Input

- Provide positive reinforcement and additional ideas to try for each coach.

Addition of Other Techniques to the List

- See if the volunteers have other points to add to their list of techniques based on their practice experience.

Questions and Answers

- Encourage participants to ask questions to clarify and extend their understanding of the coaching process.

Note: It is a good idea to reproduce the list of tips that the group generated so that each coach may have a copy for reference.

Joanne C. Wachter, *Classroom Volunteers: Uh-Oh! or Right On!* Copyright © 1999, Corwin Press, Inc.

REPRODUCIBLE 11

Planning Frame for Training Editors

Warm-Up

- Welcome participants.
- Give each volunteer a card with a comment such as:
  - Grammar and spelling are the most important part of learning to write.
  - Grammar and spelling are not that important as long as you can understand the meaning of what was written.
  - Children should be given lots of time to write in their own way before formal spelling and grammar are imposed on them.
  - Youngsters should learn the correct way to write from the beginning or they will acquire bad habits.
- Give the volunteers 3 to 5 minutes to talk with a partner about their reactions to their cards.
- Debrief the activity by talking about the district's or school's philosophy regarding instruction on language mechanics. Beware! This can be an emotional issue for many people, so be ready to explain the philosophy with clarity and conviction. Also, save yourself and your volunteers distress by choosing editors who are in tune with your program.

Discussion of Skills That Participants Will Acquire

- Ability to decide how to review papers for language mechanics
- Knowledge of the way to mark areas for improvement
- Ability to communicate with youngsters about editing

Joanne C. Wachter, *Classroom Volunteers: Uh-Oh! or Right On!* Copyright © 1999, Corwin Press, Inc.

REPRODUCIBLE 11 (continued)

Modeling of How to Mark Papers

- Put up an overhead transparency of a child's writing that includes some language mechanics and spelling errors.
- Talk through how you would choose three types of errors on which to focus so as not to overwhelm or discourage the child.
- Demonstrate how you would mark these areas for growth in a positive, constructive way.

Demonstration of Editing Conference

- Have a teacher conduct an editing conference with a child.

Discussion of Skills Observed

- Engage participants in a conversation about how the teacher focused on a manageable number of editing skills.
- Ask participants to identify techniques the teacher used to preserve the child's dignity and maintain his or her interest and confidence in writing.

Practice

- Give pairs of participants papers to mark and prepare for conferences.
- Have participants either conduct editing conferences with the authors of their papers or role-play conferences with each other.

Input From Observers

- Encourage partners to compliment each other on successes and make suggestions for ideas to try in the future.

Closure

- Engage participants in creating a "do's and don'ts" list for Editors. Copy and distribute the list to all "graduates" of the workshop.

Joanne C. Wachter, *Classroom Volunteers: Uh-Oh! or Right On!* Copyright © 1999, Corwin Press, Inc.

REPRODUCIBLE 12

Planning Frame for Training Reading Coaches

Warm-Up

- Give participants a difficult piece of text to read. It could be a passage full of educational jargon or an excerpt from a medical journal, for instance. Ask participants to try to read and comprehend the passage, noticing the techniques they use when they have trouble. After a few minutes of reading time, engage the group in a discussion of how they felt, what they tried to do to help themselves, and how these strategies worked.

What the Participants Will Gain From the Session

- Understanding of what to do to set up a reading session with a child
- Skills they can use with a child who encounters trouble when reading

Observing the Set-Up for a Reading Session

- Take the participants to a primary-grade class where the teacher or another person who has had training in how to read with a child is introducing a youngster to a new story. Upon returning from the experience, put up an overhead that describes story introduction steps and ask participants how they saw these elements used.
  - Setting the child at ease with informal conversation
  - Sitting so that both the child and the coach can easily see the book
  - Asking the child to look at the cover and title and do a picture walk to make predictions about the content of the book

Presenting Tips on What to Do When a Child Makes an Error

- Explain that errors help coaches see what a child already knows and what he or she is ready to learn next. Hand out and go over a chart of actions to take for each kind of error.

Joanne C. Wachter, *Classroom Volunteers: Uh-Oh! or Right On!* Copyright © 1999, Corwin Press, Inc.

REPRODUCIBLE 12 (continued)

Error	Appropriate Response
The child makes an error that doesn't affect the meaning ("He went into his HOME," instead of "He went into his house").	Say nothing at the time of the error. Return to the word after the child has finished the story and help work it out.
The child comes to a word, stops cold, and can't predict what it is.	Ask the child to guess a word that would make sense based on what has been read so far. Help the child check the guess against the letters in the word to see if the guess is correct. If not, try again.
The child makes an error that affects meaning and becomes confused ("He went to his horse" instead of "He went to his house").	Coach the child to go back to the beginning of the sentence and read it again. If that doesn't help, ask him or her to read to the end of the sentence and see if that helps.
The child makes an error that affects meaning and keeps on going.	Stop and ask if what he or she read makes sense. When the child realizes it doesn't, follow the steps in the previous tip.
The story is too hard, and the child makes so many errors that it is not making sense.	Read the story to the child and ask him or her to chime in with you when he or she can. Reread it and see if the child can read more the second time with your help.

Source: From Joanne C. Strohmer (Wachter) and Clare Carhart, *Time-Saving Tips for Teachers*, p. 109. Copyright © 1997 by Corwin Press, Inc.

Observing Coaching Skills in Use

- Give teachers a chance to observe and discuss a live demonstration or tape of a coach and child working through errors.

Practicing the Techniques

- Because this is a role that requires more expertise than some others, it is important to provide several practice and feedback sessions for coaches.

Joanne C. Wachter, *Classroom Volunteers: Uh-Oh! or Right On!* Copyright © 1999, Corwin Press, Inc.

REPRODUCIBLE 13

Planning Frame for Training Book Discussion Facilitators

Warm-Up

- Engage participants in discussing a recent movie that most have seen. As they talk, unobtrusively jot down the kinds of information they are discussing. After the conversation dies down, point out that none of them engaged in a "school" discussion involving anyone asking questions such as, "Who was the main character?"

What Participants Will Learn

- How to start a book discussion
- When to step in and when to step back and let youngsters lead
- Technique for debriefing a book discussion

(Volunteers will be successful only if you have the children well trained in book discussion before they work with the coach.)

Present Tips for Facilitating a Book Discussion

- Start with an open-ended question such as: What did you think of this story? or Did the story remind you of any other book or anything that has ever happened to you or anyone you know?
- Let children lead with the points they have prepared to bring up in discussion.
- Jump into the conversation only when discussion has dried up and you have waited 10 seconds to see if anyone else restarts it. If it is necessary for you to say something, use another open-ended question or comment such as, "What did you find confusing or hard to understand?"
- While discussion is under way, jot down notes about how each child contributed.

Demonstration

- Invite participants to sit as silent observers of a book discussion. Have them take notes about what they see and jot down questions.

Joanne C. Wachter, *Classroom Volunteers: Uh-Oh! or Right On!* Copyright © 1999, Corwin Press, Inc.

REPRODUCIBLE 13 (continued)

Discussion of Demonstration

- After the demonstration, give participants plenty of time to comment on their observations and ask questions.

Practice

- Give each participant a short piece of literature to read.
- Have participants work in pairs to decide how they might start the discussion and what kinds of restart questions or comments they might have ready, if needed.

Share and Provide Peer and Presenter Feedback

- Allocate some time to sharing the results of the partner work.

REPRODUCIBLE 14

Mini-Lesson Frame

Objective: Children will demonstrate the ability to use the following productive behaviors when working with a volunteer teacher:

_____

_____

Modeling: The following suggestions can help children get a clear picture of the desired behaviors for working with a volunteer.

_____ Role-play by you and a child of inappropriate and appropriate ways of handling situations that could arise with volunteer staff

_____ Skit by children who have had the chance to prepare a presentation showing the target appropriate behavior for working with a volunteer helper

_____ Teacher demonstration with "think alouds" (talking through the behavior choices and the reasons for them)

_____ Pictures, drawn by students, of the behavior they wish to discuss

_____ Relevant literature selections to be read and followed by discussion of wise and unwise behavior choices

_____ Film or video clips that show the expected behaviors in action followed by discussion

_____ Entertaining demonstrations of behavior with a volunteer by older children or adults (what to and what not to do)

_____ Observation of a demonstration followed by brainstorming a list of guidelines to use when faced with situations involving peer pressure when a volunteer teacher is working with a child

_____ Other _____

_____

_____

Joanne C. Wachter, *Classroom Volunteers: Uh-Oh! or Right On!* Copyright © 1999, Corwin Press, Inc.

REPRODUCIBLE 14 (continued)

Guided Practice: Give youngsters a chance to practice target behaviors with your coaching. Choose one of the following:

_____ Practice with a partner.

_____ Rehearse with a small group.

_____ Have students demonstrate in front of the class and receive peer response.

_____ Provide information about an authentic application of the behavior and ask youngsters to explain in their journals what they would do.

_____ Other _____

Independent Practice: When youngsters will be working with volunteers, remind them to be aware of the target behavior. Tell them that you will be asking them to think about their observations and experiences when the volunteer finishes his or her work for the day and leaves.

Self-Assessment: Invite children to think back on their experiences with the volunteer and consider how they performed related to the objective. Use one of the following activities after providing 2 to 3 minutes of private "thinking time" for them to reflect.

_____ Complete a journal entry explaining when they used the behavior and how they thought it worked. (Perhaps, pair with a classmate and exchange ideas.)

_____ Facilitate a class discussion of instances involving the behavior and the pluses and minuses of the performance.

REPRODUCIBLE 14 (continued)

_____ Complete a simple self-evaluation form or individual contract such as the one below.

Name _____

Behavior _____

How did I do? _____

    ___ Great

    ___ Making progress

    ___ Still need to practice

Other comments: _____

_____ Other _____

_____

_____

Closure: Congratulate the youngsters on their progress in learning the target behavior. Comment on additional ways that they can practice and develop the skill the next time they work with a volunteer.

Source: Lesson adapted from Dori E. Novak and Joanne C. Strohmer (Wachter), *You Don't Have to Dread Cafeteria Duty*, pp. 87-88. Copyright © 1998 by Corwin Press, Inc.

REPRODUCIBLE 15

How Did We Do?

What makes us proud of how we worked with _____?	What do we want to do even better next time?

Joanne C. Wachter, *Classroom Volunteers: Uh-Oh! or Right On!* Copyright © 1999, Corwin Press, Inc.

REPRODUCIBLE 16

Task and Response Sheet for Writing Coach

Date _____   Writing Coach _____

Task

Please work with _____

Writing skill(s) to focus on: _____

Comments:

Results

Writing Concepts Reference List

    Using plans
    Getting ideas down in a rough draft
    Starting a piece in an interesting way
    Organizing the ideas
    Including details to make the writing understandable and interesting
    Ending the piece in an interesting way

Some things he/she understands well:

Something new I noticed he/she is starting to learn:

A couple of concepts he/she does not yet understand:

Joanne C. Wachter, *Classroom Volunteers: Uh-Oh! or Right On!* Copyright © 1999, Corwin Press, Inc.

REPRODUCIBLE 17

Task and Response Sheet for Editor

Date _____   Editor _____

Task

Please work with _____

Editing skill(s) to focus on: _____

Comments:

Results

Editing Concepts Reference List

    Specific capitalization conventions
    Particular types of punctuation
    Certain spelling patterns
    Grammar and usage conventions

Some concepts he/she understands well:

A concept he/she is just starting to understand:

A couple of concepts he/she still needs to learn:

Joanne C. Wachter, *Classroom Volunteers: Uh-Oh! or Right On!* Copyright © 1999, Corwin Press, Inc.

REPRODUCIBLE 18

Task and Response Sheet for Reading Coach

Date _____   Reading Coach _____

Task

Please listen to _____

Especially notice _____

Comments:

Results

Focus Strategies Reference List

    Paying attention to the letters when trying to figure out a word
    Paying attention to whether what he/she is reading makes sense
    Going back to correct him/herself when something does not make sense
    Retelling the big ideas of the piece he/she read
    Other:

Some things he/she did well:

Something I worked on with him/her:

A couple of concepts or skills he/she still needs to learn:

Joanne C. Wachter, *Classroom Volunteers: Uh-Oh! or Right On!* Copyright © 1999, Corwin Press, Inc.

REPRODUCIBLE 19

Task and Response Sheet for Discussion Facilitators

Date _____ Discussion Facilitator _____

Selection being discussed _____

Names of participants   *Comments about participation*

_____   _____

_____   _____

_____   _____

_____   _____

_____   _____

Kinds of discussion

_____ Traits of characters

_____ Impact of setting on the selection

_____ Events in the selection

_____ Techniques the author used

_____ How the selection relates to their lives

_____ Connections between the selection and other stories

Quality of interaction

_____ No one dominated.

_____ Everyone was included.

_____ Participants were respectful of others' views.

_____ Individuals backed up their opinions with details from the story.

Other comments on the discussion experience:

Joanne C. Wachter, *Classroom Volunteers: Uh-Oh! or Right On!* Copyright © 1999, Corwin Press, Inc.

REPRODUCIBLE 20

Task and Response Sheet for Travel Agents

Date _____ Travel Agent _____

Tasks accomplished since our last communication:

Tasks   Comments/Explanations

_____   _____

_____   _____

_____   _____

_____   _____

_____   _____

What still needs to be done related to:

_____ Transportation   _____

_____ Communication with location _____

_____ Permission slips   _____

_____ Eating arrangements   _____

_____ Other   _____

_____ Other   _____

_____ Other   _____

_____ Other   _____

_____ Other   _____

_____ Other   _____

_____ Other   _____

_____ Other   _____

Joanne C. Wachter, *Classroom Volunteers: Uh-Oh! or Right On!* Copyright © 1999, Corwin Press, Inc.

REPRODUCIBLE 21

Task and Response Sheet for Secretary

Date _____   Secretary _____

Tasks accomplished since our last communication:

Tasks   Comments/Explanations

_____   _____
_____   _____
_____   _____
_____   _____
_____   _____

What still needs to be done related to:

_____ Phone calls   _____
_____ Letters/notes   _____
_____ Copying   _____
_____ Preparing handouts   _____
_____ Other   _____
_____ Other   _____
_____ Other   _____
_____ Other   _____
_____ Other   _____
_____ Other   _____
_____ Other   _____
_____ Other   _____

Joanne C. Wachter, *Classroom Volunteers: Uh-Oh! or Right On!* Copyright © 1999, Corwin Press, Inc.

REPRODUCIBLE 22

Shopping List

Get From School Storage	Buy at a store	Item	Get From School Storage	Buy at a store	Item
_____	_____	Staples	_____	_____	Paper clips
_____	_____	Pencils	_____	_____	Rubber bands
_____	_____	Lines paper	_____	_____	Art paper
_____	_____	Crayons	_____	_____	Paints
_____	_____	Chalk	_____	_____	Stick-on notes
_____	_____	Copy masters	_____	_____	Thumb tacks
_____	_____	Folders	_____	_____	Index cards
_____	_____	Legal Pads	_____	_____	Notepads
_____	_____	Markers	_____	_____	Pens
_____	_____	Overhead transparencies			

Other Supplies:

Item	Location
_____	_____
_____	_____
_____	_____
_____	_____
_____	_____

Other notes about supplies:

Source: From Joanne C. Strohmer (Wachter) and Clare Carhart, *Time-Saving Tips for Teachers,* p. 62. Copyright © 1997 by Corwin Press, Inc.

Joanne C. Wachter, *Classroom Volunteers: Uh-Oh! or Right On!* Copyright © 1999, Corwin Press, Inc.

REPRODUCIBLE 23

Bulletin Board Artist's Planning Sheet

Rough sketch of art and lettering:

Exact wording to appear:

Location of supplies:

Source: From Joanne C. Strohmer (Wachter) and Clare Carhart, *Time-Saving Tips for Teachers*, p. 115. Copyright © 1997 by Corwin Press, Inc.

REPRODUCIBLE 24

Volunteer End-of-the-Year Survey

Please take a few moments to answer the following questions.

1. What did you like most about your role as _____? Why?

2. Is there any additional training that would be helpful in this role?

3. What might be some suggestions for making the program run even better next year?

4. Is there any other role you would like to try if the opportunity becomes available? What about this role interests you?

Joanne C. Wachter, *Classroom Volunteers: Uh-Oh! or Right On!* Copyright © 1999, Corwin Press, Inc.

REPRODUCIBLE 25

About Our Classroom Helpers

Please answer the questions.

1. What did you like about working with our volunteer helpers this year?

2. If you were a teacher, what would you tell volunteer helpers about working with children?

3. What are some other things that helpers might do in our classroom?

Joanne C. Wachter, *Classroom Volunteers: Uh-Oh! or Right On!* Copyright © 1999, Corwin Press, Inc.

In compliance with GPSR, should you have any concerns about the safety of this product, please advise: International Associates Auditing & Certification Limited The Black Church, St Mary's Place, Dublin 7, D07 P4AX Ireland
EUAR@ie.ia-net.com